THOUGHT CATALOG BOOKS

Orlando

Orlando

A Series Of Diverse Voices On Guns, Homophobia, And Surviving Hatred

JACOB GEERS

THOUGHT CATALOG BOOKS

Brooklyn, NY

Contents

Introduction   1

1. I Stand With Love   3
    —*Kendra Syrdal*

2. Here Are All The People Applauding The Orlando Gay   9
    Club Shooter
    —*Jacob Geers*

3. Orlando Shooting Proves Fight For LGBTQ+ Rights Is Far,   19
    Far From Over
    —*Nick Prayner*

4. 'What I Saw There Was Amazing,' Woman Says About   21
    Donating Blood In Orlando The Day Of The Attack

5. In This Time Of Hate, We Must Turn To Love   25
    —*Allison Hope*

6. This Is My Apology For Rejecting Gay Pride Until Today   29
    —*Steven Nolan*

7. I Am A Queer Muslim And Please Remember That   33
    Terrorism Isn't Tied To Faith
    —*Hannah Mesouani*

8. A European's Perspective On The Orlando Shooting And   37
    U.S. Gun Control
    —*Melisa Ergin*

9. To All My Queer Friends, Here's What Our Straight   41
    Friends Won't Tell Us About The Orlando Attack
    —*Justin Taroli*

10. Orlando Isn't Just An LGBT Tragedy, It's All Of Ours   45
    —*Chelsea Forbes-Terry*

11. Stop Telling LGBTQ People How We Should Be   49
Responding To The Orlando Attack
—Mitch King

12. Here Is What The Manager Of Pulse Nightclub Had To Say   53
About The Attack
—Jacob Geers

13. Why Gay Nightclubs Are Such Necessary Places Of   55
Survival To The LGBTQ Community
—Madison Moore

14. I'm Tired Of Watching Humans Die Just Because Some   59
People Really, Really Like Their Guns
—Jacob Geers

15. Those Who Are Missed. Those Who Are Remembered.   65
—Jacob Geers

Introduction

In the early morning of Sunday, June 12th a terrorist by the name of Omar Mateen stormed into Orlando's Pulse Nightclub and opened fire on dozens of patrons. Running for their lives, guests tried to escape the bloodshed. Some managed — while others did not. By the time police apprehended the gunman, 1 in 3 of the people who were at Pulse at the start of the shooting were either dead or injured.

How do we deal with this? How do we get up every day and know that this evil exists, just waiting to tear us down? How do we process these senseless acts of violence?

This book doesn't have the answers to those questions. This book doesn't reveal a hidden meaning or missing insight behind this heinous attack. This book doesn't explain why Omar Mateen committed this horrific crime — be it his upbringing, his possible connections with terror groups, his religion, his self-hate for being gay himself, or some other equally horrendous reason.

What this book does — or at least hopes to do — is provide a context to discuss hate and violence in our country. A collection of different essays — by authors of all different backgrounds, colors, faiths, and sexualities — stand together in trying to discuss where we go in this age of senseless slaughter, and how we endure through senseless violence and toxic hate.

This book can't stand alone, however. We all have to be a part of this conversation and a part of the solution. You don't have to agree with everything said here — indeed, we would prefer if you didn't. But we do have to be bold enough to have a civil national and global dialogue about what drives hate, bigotry, and terrorism. Hopefully this is the start of that dialogue: a discussion not tethered by dogmas, but one liberated by honesty, understanding, and compassion. After all, we are all in this together.

Peace,
Jacob Geers

1

I Stand With Love

Kendra Syrdal

This morning I woke up and like millions of other people, I was shocked and devastated to hear that the deadliest mass shooting in US history took place in the early hours of the morning at Pulse nightclub.

Around 2 in the morning in Orlando, Florida, Omar Mateen stormed the gay nightclub with an assault rifle, a handgun, and another device and opened fire. He held club patrons hostage until 5 AM before being taken down in a shootout with police. He was a licensed security officer with a concealed weapons permit in the state of Florida and had been previously listed as a person of interest with the the FBI.

50 people were reported dead with 53 more seriously injured following the attack.

People are calling it an act of terrorism, Islamic this Islamic that.

But let's call it what it really was.

This was a direct, methodical, organized attack on marginalized, LGBT+ people.

This was a hate crime.

I do not claim to know Omar Mateen's religion or political ideology. And frankly, I don't think either of those things matter. I do think that this is yet another tragic example of how little we've been doing in regards to solving the issue of gun violence in America but I think there is another problem at hand.

And Omar Mateen's political alignment and religious beliefs are not the problem.

Because I 100% believe that he localized his attack towards members of the LGBT community because their mere existence made him angry. His own father said that his homophobic reaction to seeing two men kissing was to be filled with rage. So who or whatever he prayed to in the morning or at night, and who or whatever he believed politically in doesn't really matter.

What matters is that he was hateful.

And *that's* a problem.

Hatred is a poison. It seeps into you and attacks your heart and your soul and wraps itself around you until it calls the shots. Hatred solves nothing. It ruins everything.

Hatred kills.

How awful is that? That your hatred for someone just breathing the same air as you and being different sparks that much hate in your heart?

I grew up in a place where being gay or different was absolutely abnormal. I grew up listening to my godmother talk about gay men and use words like "disgusting" and "sinful" to describe them. I grew up listening to people at my family's church preach about going to hell for being interested in someone of the same sex and where someone simply dressing outside of the gender norm was ostracized and talked about in the nastiest of ways. I grew up being told to not mention my best friend's sexuality when I came home from college around specific family members. I still get into heated "discussions" when I go back because it's not something that understood or accepted but at 26 I refuse to tiptoe around their ignorance anymore.

But it always made (and continues to make) my stomach turn.

Just thinking about it now makes my throat tighten and my heartbeat start to elevate.

And why is that? Why is my body's reaction to this sort of talk, this warped way of thinking, and ideology to instantly reject it?

Because hatred shouldn't be natural, ignored, or accepted. It should make you physically uncomfortable.

But when presented with this hate I do not think the answer is to respond with hate. Fighting hate with hate gets nowhere. And giving into hate is exactly what a hateful person wants.

They want you too to be poisoned. They want your soul to be as tainted as their own.

Which is why I reject hate, and completely, fully, totally, and unapologetically embrace love.

I stand with those who love.

I stand with those who are unafraid to be themselves. I stand with those who look into the face of hatred and bigotry and refuse to become like that. I stand with people who say, "This is who I am and I love myself." I stand with everyone who has been told they are not okay and they are not wanted and they are not normal but continue to march and fight for equality and the ability to love not only themselves, but whoever else.

I do not stand with hate.

I will never stand with hate.

I stand with love.

And today, in the face of utter tragedy, on a day where "deadliest mass shooting" is ringing in my ears, weighing heavy on my heart, and making so many people that I love afraid, it is more important than ever to align myself (and *yourself*) with love.

Love is louder than hate. Love is more powerful than hate. Love will do MORE than hate.

Hatred spits, but Love welcomes. Hatred is exhausting, but

Love is rejuvenating. Hatred belittles, but Love is uplifting. Hatred judges, but Love is open. Hatred ruins, but Love rebuilds.

Hatred kills, but Love survives.

I stand with love.

I stand with love.

(One more time for the people in the back...)

I stand with love.

And I pray that you do too.

2

Here Are All The People Applauding The Orlando Gay Club Shooter

Jacob Geers

As you probably know, last night there was a brutal hate attack on Pulse nightclub in Orlando, Florida. A terrorist by the name of Omar Saddiqui Mateen stormed the club, and opened fire on the attendees. Some were held hostage, before law enforcement was finally able to take him down. Dozens are dead, and reports are coming in that some are so badly disfigured from the gun attack, that is proving challenging to identify the bodies.

While information is still coming in, political debates about guns, religion, and sexual orientation have already cropped up. The shooter is alleged to be Muslim, and many Trump supporters are using this attack to vindicate their point. Others are trying to argue that the shooter was a Democrat, and saying that liberals are to blame for this. And other still — and most shockingly — are trivializing the attack because of the sexual orientation of the victims:

1.

Jonathan Howell
@Jhowell1214

⚙   👤+ Follow

Florida Pulse gay club attacked I'm so happy
someone decided to start shooting perverts
instead of innocent people.

Twitter

2.

WNTN
@Wontage

⚙   👤+ Follow

50 gay people died in a nightclub thats what you
call an effective shooting good shit gays dont
deserve to live

RETWEETS   LIKES
3   3

7:29 AM - 12 Jun 2016

↩   ↻ 3   ⋛   ♥ 3   •••

Twitter

3.

Pkay
@peterkaweesi
⚙ ♙ Follow

The only good thing about the Orlando Shooting is that it was a gay club. So less gays in the world today.

6:01 AM - 12 Jun 2016

Twitter

4.

Chaasad Amath
@AhchNach
⚙ ♙ Follow

I wake up to some dude shooting up a gay nightclub. Isn't that weird. Homosexuality is condemned by God so that's why he let that happen ppl

7:34 AM - 12 Jun 2016

Twitter

5.

 **WBCVideo**
@WBCVideo

God opened His armory to deal with proud fag america. 20 dead in mass shooting at #Orlando "gay" nightclub #Pulse

 **Westboro: God Sent The Shooter**
Which shooter? All shooters, apparently. The crazies at Westboro Baptist Church explain why they hold the sign "God Sent The Shooter." It's sick, I know, but...
youtube.com

RETWEETS   LIKE
6   1

6:44 AM - 12 Jun 2016

↩   ♺ 6   ≋   ♥ 1   ...

Twitter

6.

 **Dawla islamiya**
@VoiceofMuslims2

♢   ⚠ Follow

I as an individual would congratulate and give thump up to the brother who killed filthy gays at #orlando shooting

8:20 AM - 12 Jun 2016

↩   ♺   ≋   ♥   ...

Twitter

7.

Don Juan ☼ 👤 Follow
@Jesushatesfig

Man I don't know what's better that fact that
gays were killed or the fact that the killer was
Muslim and a Democrat. 😂 😂 😂 #Orlando
#Shooting

7:57 AM - 12 Jun 2016

↩   ⇄   ⩦   ♡   ⋯

Twitter

8.

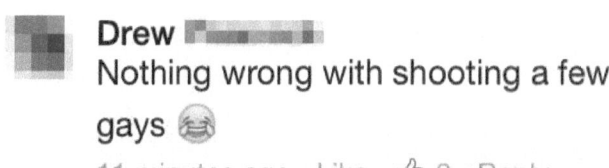

Drew ▯▬▬▮▬▮
Nothing wrong with shooting a few
gays 😂

11 minutes ago · Like · 👍 2 · Reply

Facebook

9.

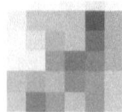

Isaac ▮▮▮▮
That is the right target for such shootings. Gays should be shot for disrespecting the natural order.

3 minutes ago · Like · 👍 2 · Reply

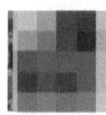

Hanif ▮▮▮▮
Gay night club?? Just disgusting and I think that gunman done a good job

13 minutes ago · Edited · Like · 👍 5 · Reply

Facebook

10.

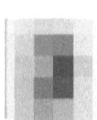

Khalid ▮▮▮▮▮
Gay people are Sick.

5 minutes ago · Like · Reply

11.

Keepin' it Real
@StukaHans

☼ 👤⁺ Follow

@DailyMail @MailOnline OK... At least it was only gays. Not like they add anything to mankind: Except disease - bit of a non - story really

5:00 AM - 12 Jun 2016

◆ West Bromwich, England

↩ ⇄ ≋ ♡ ...

Twitter

12.

Vitor
@OnlyFunIfURun

☼ 👤⁺ Follow

At least it was just gays this time and not innocent people 😂 😂 #PrayForFlorida

8:24 AM - 12 Jun 2016

↩ ⇄ ≋ ♥ ...

Twitter

13.

Oloruntoba ▮▮▮▮
The shooter is my hero, the cops should be sued for killing a hero,who was doing social justice, i mean since 80% of Americans no longer have brain's to know that homosexuality is a great sin against God and every natural human law,let those who knows please buy guns and kill off any gay,lesbian,transgender and their likes,including bruce Jenner or whatever he calls himself now.may the soul of the shooter rest in perfect peace,amen,and fyi i am a Christian not a Muslim, and my religion strongly condemns any acts of homosexuality

8 minutes ago · Like · Reply

Facebook

14.

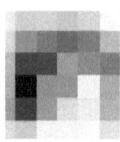

Michael ▮▮▮▮ ▮
Sinners being taken out by sin
39 minutes ago · Like · 👍 1 · Reply

15.

Karen
man should not lie with another man as a woman. it is an abomination.
This was God's hand. and he will pluck them away one by one. I have no judgement on what others do but God does.

45 minutes ago · Like · Reply

16.

Ray
To me they should filled all gays bars and blow em away. Maybe parents should really do their job and teach their child how to become men and women.,Nobody is born gay .They are made by their own parent. You got a boy teach how to become a men ,you got a girl teach how to become a woman.

Just now · Like · Reply

These people are an important part of this conversation, because they show why gay pride still needs to exist. Just because the United States has achieved marriage equality does not mean our struggle to live, laugh, and love freely is over.

These tweets and comments leave me without words. Except to say that it will get better — it must get better — and hopefully, with awareness, education, and love, the world we leave our children will be a little brighter.

3

Orlando Shooting Proves Fight For LGBTQ+ Rights Is Far, Far From Over

Nick Prayner

This morning, I was beyond disheartened to hear about the tragedy that took place in Orlando, Florida at Pulse Orlando last night, less than a year since the historic ruling of Obergefell v. Hodges on June 26th, 2015.

Fifty casualties and fifty-three more hospitalized. The deadliest mass shooting in American history. At a gay club. During Pride weekend. This is no coincidence, ladies and gentlemen. We are still targets.

The deadliest mass shooting in American history, as of this morning, is a targeted attack on the LGBTQ community.

This country needs to get a grip on reality and understand that we have not progressed for LGBTQ men, women, and non-binary folks nearly as much as we would like to believe. Trans people (especially trans women and trans women of color) are being murdered at an unfathomable rate, between 20% and 40% of the 1.6 million homeless youth in this country identify as LGBTQ, and LGBTQ men are still unable to donate blood when our own brothers and sisters need it most.

Between the mass shooting that transpired last night and the unfortunate tragedy of Joey LaBute in Columbus recently, I'm sick to my stomach and scared for my people. At this point, I'm not sure if I want to know how many more bodies there needs to be for our country to make swift, sustainable change to curb gun violence as well as the disproportionate gun violence towards marginalized people. For too long has our country turned a blind eye to the relentless attacks on members of the LGBTQ community for centuries, and we cannot afford to waste another minute brushing it off of our shoulders.

At the very fucking least, I want to be able to go to a gay bar, one of the few spaces we have left for us, without the worry that I might not make it back home alive.

Stop killing us.

4

'What I Saw There Was Amazing,' Woman Says About Donating Blood In Orlando The Day Of The Attack

As many of you probably know at this point, last night there was a horrific terrorist attack on a gay club in Orlando, Florida.

And while all of us — from all over the world — have felt the story weigh on our heart, there is one Orlando-based girl who decided she had to take action.

The woman, Carolyn Gavin, made her way to one of the blood drives where she hoped to give her donation (She was ultimately asked to come back later in the week). But it was what she saw there that truly moved her:

In her own words:

> *In light of the horrific shootings in downtown Orlando early this morning, everyone who is able was urged to donate blood. I went to one of the blood drives today since I am one of the blood types that they so desperately need. What I saw when I was there was one of the most amazing things that I have ever seen in my entire life. When we arrived, there was a FIVE HOUR line to donate blood. Five hours. That is the most incredible thing. They said that everyone was welcome to wait in line, but they might run out of supplies before the line was finished. People had driven hours to donate blood so they waited. Others, who were local like myself, were asked if they would like to sign up to donate later in the week when they were in a greater need again.*
>
> *Instead of just leaving once we signed up to donate later in the week, my friend and I stayed to help as we could and to observe the magic that was taking place with so many different people coming together to help as much as*

they could. We helped unload a huge, seven-seater SUV that was completely filled with packs of bottled water. Every, single nook and cranny of that car had a pack of water in it. And that family had two other cars with them full of water, other drinks, and snacks for the blood bank. The generosity of not only this family, but every person who donated today is so wonderful. Seeing people come together is the real magic that we have in this world.

Facebook

For darkness to succeed, it must extinguish every flicker of light. Clearly, despite the despair and tragedy, it has failed in Orlando.

5

In This Time Of Hate, We Must Turn To Love

Allison Hope

News of another act of hate, this time a man who opened fire in a nightclub, took many lives and launched the country back into acute fear.

For the past at least 15 years, we have followed the same pattern. Intense shock that someone or some group could hate what Americans stand for enough to kill us; fear that it happened on our soil; and an unquestioned scramble to clamp down on the problem with decisions based in ignorance which only make matters worse.

We become more suspicious of Muslims; we allow our police forces and security agencies more leniency to spy on us all and to further militarize our lives. We give rise to people like Donald Trump who say terribly dangerous things that divide and marginalize us, which only lead to more attacks.

News reports follow the same pattern when reporting this as they have others — this man, Omar Mateen, acted on his own. But, much like the couple in San Bernardino, they were connected to a larger group and ideology that is very scary. This is not a disgruntled high school student. But the results are the same. People are dead. The country is tuned in. We are scared.

We feel like victims, but the truth is that we created the terrifying reality we now know.

This brand of terrorism is only just getting started. Anyone born before 9/11 has not known what it's like to grow up with war in our own streets. We are now living in a time when our neighborhoods are battlegrounds.

The problem was exacerbated when George W. Bush stepped in front of the camera to look at the vulnerable, tear-stained American public reeling from the fall of two towers and thousands dead, and said two horribly wrong things:

1. We must buy cars and shop to keep the economy running
2. We're going to kill the son of a bitch that did this to us

In both instances, he was fueling the very hatred that spawned terrorist groups like ISIS, and teaching the public that consumerism and violence were American values. Neither will ever help us heal.

Toni Morrison stood tall in that moment and pointed a finger at our President. She said what he failed to say was that we should turn and hug our families. In fact, what I think we need at this time more than ever, and what we've failed to do time and again, is to hug our neighbors and spread love to smother the hate.

We need to hold interfaith events in our communities and get to know our Muslim neighbors, our gay neighbors, our black neighbors. We need to lay down our arms and our ignorant biases and not let our fear guide our policies.

We need to teach our children that violence and hate are wrong, and that difference is something to embrace.

We need to make deadly weapons less readily available and keep them out of the hands of our kids. We need better access to mental health services and health care. We need to stop killing other people in other countries for vague reasons. And we need to stop thinking that we're somehow better than anyone else.

"This is not the America I thought I'd find myself and my children and grandchildren in," Tom Brokov said on Meet the Press. He urged us to take a deep breath and mourn and act rationally.

I'm terrified to think about raising a child in today's world. Let's lead the way back towards the light. It's not too late.

6

This Is My Apology For Rejecting Gay Pride Until Today

Steven Nolan

I'm ashamed to admit that up until today I was disgusted by Pride parades. The images in my mind of shirtless men in speedos, drag queens performing outrageously, and public displays of affection made me want to disaffiliate my own community.

"No wonder people don't take gays seriously when they act like this," I complained all too frequently.

What I failed to realize was that their unapologetic celebration of their sexualities was not hedonism, nor for pleasure alone. **It took 50 innocent souls dying for me to recognize that Pride is bravery.**

Every single member of the LGBTQ+ community who attends Pride makes a radical statement without saying anything. By publicly identifying as a member of this community, each person puts himself or herself at risk. These dangers don't always mean a tragic mass shooting — though this is the most strikingly painful example of them. Sometimes attending Pride means risking being ostracized by your family if a photo surfaces online. Sometimes attending Pride means peacefully ignoring hateful slurs from protestors, as my friend Emery experienced while volunteering in Nashville. By attending Pride, these brothers and sisters show that they are not afraid of the consequences, and even if they do have fears, their courage is stronger.

At Pride, nobody is trying to hide, and that made me uncomfortable. Rather than compulsively attempting to blend into a heteronormative society, Pride flaunts homosexuality.

What I saw as disgraceful or trashy is actually a bold subversion, a shameless expression that demands for recognition. The point is to be "in your face" for a day or a week or a month of the year, and I apologize for not appreciating that.

For as long as I can remember, I've strived to be as "inoffensive" as possible. I've frequently told others and myself, "I am more than my sexuality" and believed I was doing so to remain authentic. Whether in my dress, mannerisms, interests, or actions, I've made sure to distance myself from what I perceive as the typical homosexual. I always assumed that by never going "too far" I'd never be at too much of a risk, sort of like how Cam and Mitch remain hilarious and palatable for most television viewers because they're virtually sexless.

For the first time, I recognize how wrong I am. I see that my rejection of Pride was somewhat of an apology for my sexuality, if not an outright rejection of it.

To all those who celebrated and mourned across the country this weekend and especially to those who lost your lives, I apologize and thank you for your courage. I promise I'll be out there with you next year.

7

I Am A Queer Muslim And Please Remember That Terrorism Isn't Tied To Faith

Hannah Mesouani

I'm a queer Muslim. To those of you who think that's an oxymoron look no further than the motto, "land of the free, home of the brave." **It feels like those who are not free are the only members of this nation who are showing any kind of bravery; whilst the free, for the most part, hide behind a veil of privilege.**

What happened in Orlando was absolutely horrifying and indicative of systemic hate and oppression. The media response from the "powers that be" was nothing short of disgusting (I'm looking at you Trump). No one should be congratulated over the death of the innocent. One wife-beating asshole does not represent an entire faith.

To those of you who do not think that homophobia is

real, look no further. To those of you who do not think gun control is an issue, look at the numbers.

To take an instance of homophobia and turn it into a religious war only does more to belittle the lives of a community who have fought for decades to fall in love and build honest lives together — without you peeking up their skirts or preaching fire and brimstone. The massacre at Pulse was not about Islam. It's not about the immigration the media would have you believe — the night of the shooting was a Latin night whose flyer featured beautiful, strong trans women in celebration.

These are the victims, a people as deserving of a home here as any of you. Brown bodies wanting to be free and find joy, only to be gunned down by a lone killer who let society and a twisted view of faith affirm his view that these poor souls were lesser. They are not. We are not. We are most certainly not better if we do nothing to change hateful spiral we are all going down.

Stop fighting hate with hate. We need reform. Realize that to be free we must be brave, and challenge those voices that only scream oppression.

Don't let indifferent officials tell you who and how to hate. Support each other and fight to allow people both like and not like you to love each other and feel safe enough to love themselves and dance or use a bathroom in peace.

Remember those acts of horror that happen all around the

world that the media does not deem worthy enough to reach your newsfeeds. **Remember that terrorism comes in all colors and is not tied to one faith.** It happens in the policies we do nothing to change and the slurs we let slide with no qualms. Remember that your definition of family or of a man or woman is not Merriam-Webster approved and you are no one's God to deem how they should or should not live.

If you don't want to see two men in love, look the fuck away. But don't use the continued hurt of a wounded community to direct your hate elsewhere or affirm made-up truths that support your own heartless agenda.

Pray for the victims, but don't forget to be angry. Not at another group of oppressed individuals, but the people who strip these groups of agency and identity. Be mad at the politicians who want to destroy the idea of intersectional identities and crush both change and joy.

The only side you have to choose is the one of love and acceptance, not "us," not "them." Remember that families have been torn apart and devastated — families just as worthy as your own; there is no room for more hate unless it is directed at those policies that allow these things to happen. This isn't about your religious persecution or your straight cisgender discomfort at a group of beautiful people daring to be happy. An American homophobe is a terrorist regardless of whom he worships, and when you are a silent member of a country of hateful homophobes, you are part of the problem, too.

8

A European's Perspective On The Orlando Shooting And U.S. Gun Control

Melisa Ergin

30 people will be shot dead today in the United States. If it's less, tomorrow it will be more. Yesterday, 50 people were killed in the deadliest mass shooting in U.S. history.

"Guns don't kill people, humans kill people."

This is the argument that you will hear whenever you try to talk to someone who is against gun control. As a European who spent my university years in the United States, gun control was one of those controversial topics that I never really could understand. The argument that humans kill people makes sense (to some) at first glance, but it's really not that simple.

Would we be able to kill others if guns weren't so readily available? The answer is no. And this isn't just my opinion, it's a fact. Those who are pro-guns will tell you that even if the

United States had gun control this wouldn't change the number of gun related fatalities. *But it would.*

2016 marks the 20th anniversary of a mass shooting in Australia, which led to strict gun control. The chances of murder by a gun in Australia plunged 72 per cent since 1996 when gun control was introduced.

The country has had no mass shootings since. Zero.

In 2015 in the United States, there were 372 mass shootings, killing 475 and wounding 1,870 (according to the Mass Shooting Tracker). A mass shooting is defined as a single shooting incident which kills or injures four or more people, including the assailant(s).

To put this into perspective for you, the number of gun murders in the United States in 2012, was 30 times more than that in the UK.

In the UK, in 1996, 43-year-old Thomas Hamilton killed 16 five and six-year-olds, along with the teacher who tried to protect them. Handguns were effectively banned after this massacre. There has only been ONE spree killing since this one in June 2010 when a lone gunman killed 12 people before killing himself in Cumbria, England.

Let me simplify this for you, in the UK it only took *one* mass shooting (like those that occur weekly in the U.S.) for gun legislation to be passed.

So you can imagine my shock when I moved to the United

States in 2011 and witnessed news after news about mass shootings.

We are 164 days into 2016. The United States has had 133 mass shootings during this time.

A total of 207 people have died in these incidents, including those who were shot at Pulse nightclub in Orlando. In 2016, there have already been 15 mass shootings in Florida.

What's astonishing is that mass shootings only make up a fraction of America's gun violence problem. The CDC estimated that in 2013 alone, 33, 636 people died in firearm related deaths (this is 92 people every day). However, only 1.5% of these deaths (502 people) were connected to mass shootings. *How often do we hear about a five year-old child who found their father's gun and accidentally killed themselves or one of their parents?*

Just two days before the Pulse nightclub shooting in Orlando, 22-year-old singer Christina Grimmie was shot and killed in Orlando following her concert. For unknown reasons, 26-year-old Kevin James Loibl, decided to drive from St Petersburg to Orlando to kill the singer. Orlando police chief said that Liobl did not seem to have known the singer personally but speculated that he may have been a deranged fan. A deranged fan who was able to get his hands on a gun and shoot her.

These are just a few examples of the gun related horrors that face U.S. residents on a daily basis.

After the Viginia Tech shooting in 2007, we were reminded that going to college isn't safe. After the Sandy Hook shooting in 2012, we were horrified and shocked by the idea that the U.S. government thought that killing children was bearable. Today, we are confronted with what is the deadliest mass shooting in U.S. history. And yet, there are *still* people who are arguing that gun control wouldn't have changed the outcome of this incident.

This is an ongoing cycle.

Every time there is a mass shooting, there are mumbles about gun control, and then a week later this is forgotten, until the headlines of another horrific mass shooting. And then this cycle is repeated, *but nothing ever changes.*

We cannot stop these mass shootings by sitting at home and hoping that we can end hate, or hoping that maybe today someone won't walk into a gun shop with the intention to kill another human.

Humans may kill humans, but guns help them do it.

9

To All My Queer Friends, Here's What Our Straight Friends Won't Tell Us About The Orlando Attack

Justin Taroli

To all my queer friends, do not be diluted by all the straight people claiming what happened in Orlando is a "senseless" act of violence. We, as queer people, know better. This was not a senseless act. Considering the world LGBTQ people are forced to exist in, it actually makes complete sense, and we know this. This is not just about access to guns, homophobia and mental illness. People will try to make you believe this can only be about one thing, but we will never fully understand anything unless we open our minds to hate being about more than just access to a gun. Most importantly, and this is something you will not hear from your straight friends, and something you will never hear on the news: this is about self hate.

Additionally, straight people, talking heads, will try to turn us against each other. They will try to blame this on religion (which is partially involved, in some way), but the enemy here is not each other. You will hear and see straight people politicizing this and trying to turn us into some sort of cause. But do not forget your humanity in this. Do not forget to see yourself.

What no straight person will tell you, and what they will never fully see, is that you don't go into a bar and kill fifty people simply because you don't like them; you do it because part of you is them, and that part of you doesn't only hate them, that part of you hates yourself. What no straight person will tell you, and what you will never see on the news in regard to hate crimes involving sexuality, is that the answer to this does not lie within blame. The answer here is not about a gun. The answer here is dealing with repression of self.

Disagree with me all you want, but no person kills 50 queers if that person himself is not completely freaked out and frightened of his own sexuality, and this is something you will never hear on the news. The reality is this: this will continue to happen, because we, as a society, refuse to ever look inward. We, as LGBTQ people all know this first hand, because we have all had that fork in the road where we decided to love ourselves, rather than go in the opposite direction. Every one of us has had the capacity at one point or another to choose violence, and we went the other way, because we went in the direction of choosing to love ourselves.

The same reason we continue to push each other away is the same reason we kill each other in night clubs. One is just a seed, while the other is an entire fucking forest. To blame this on mental illness is taking the easy way out. To blame this all on religion is missing half the battle. To blame this all on gun laws is a step in the right direction, but it's not solving the hate we create within ourselves. It is only solving a symptom of that hate.

When a man walks into a building and decides to kill fifty people of the LGBTQ community, it is easy to be blinded by this man's hate and violence, but that is too easy. The way we rise above this is by doing something I have been telling myself my entire life: respond to hate by continuing to love. Continue being the very thing that is being hated or rejected. Take comfort in your sexuality. Relax in your intensity. It's not easy. When there is literally a mass shooting specifically aimed at who you are, I understand the need to contract. But from the time I was fourteen being severely bullied in high school for being gay, to today, where my people are actually being killed, I'll continue expanding, and I encourage all of you to do the same.

When faced with any type of adversity, my advice to everyone is to continue being more you. Being yourself, as a queer person, is in itself a form of protest, an act of rebellion. Don't let anyone tell you otherwise. I tell people this because it's all I really know, and it's what I have done my entire life. I have never been big on activism, or protesting, or any type of social justice that involves being seen in large groups. Not because it doesn't work (it often does), but because I believe greatly that none of that means anything if you can't practice it in your every day life, with the people you know and the people you meet. It creates something a bit stronger and becomes more real.

Something like this could easily make me scared of all the hate in the world, but that's too easy. Instead, this reinforces more than ever, that we need to continue believing there is good. The good does outweigh the bad, and it's not something we should forget.

We're still working on it, though. And in the end, we, as the LGBTQ community will continue looking inward, because that's what we do. We'll continue opening ourselves up, because that's the choice we have made. We will continue expanding in the face of violence and adversity because that is all we've ever known. We don't have the luxury to live any other way.

10

Orlando Isn't Just An LGBT Tragedy, It's All Of Ours

Chelsea Forbes-Terry

I sat at my computer pouring over the news and not believing my eyes. I had, like most people my age, been out on Saturday night and then had brunch on Sunday morning not thinking about anything outside of my world. I'm a fairly dialed in individual but there was no Facebook notification, no Snapchat news story, no tweet that made me aware that outside of my bubble was a tragedy. As much as social media has contributed there isn't yet a way to alert people that in someplace, somewhere else within our world, heartbreak is happening.

50 people. My head couldn't grasp it. A "gay nightclub", "young people", an act of "terrorism", "homophobia", I could visually see the words but it was as if, out of respect to my mental stability, my mind wouldn't let any of it permeate. I couldn't reflect on the fact that just last year I worked eight Gay Prides across the state of Colorado, I couldn't think about the fact that in my lifetime I had attended Prides in twenty-five different states, I wasn't able to connect with the fact that

my Facebook timeline was streaming with words of horror and disbelief because many of my friends are LGBTQ. I just wasn't able to process any of it.

That was the thing; while the outpouring of support and sympathy kept mentioning that this was a tragedy for the "LGBT community", I felt that this was a tragedy for everyone as a whole. Not every person killed in the Orlando club that night was gay. I grew up in the LGBT community, with an out and proud Lesbian mom, and just because I'm a straight women doesn't diminish how this personally affected me too. It isn't any less painful for those who have LGBT parents, or sisters & brothers, or children, or teachers, or co-workers, or friends who identify as such. For anyone who knows and loves someone who is Lesbian, Gay, Bisexual, Transgender, or Queer this is their community too, it is all of ours. This wasn't an attack simply on homosexual love, this was an attack on all love.

The morning after I started reading the updated articles, seeing the faces of those slain during the massacre and my heart began to hurt. I, like many, read about the mother who's son had texted her some of his last words and I began to cry. I cried for his mother, I cried for him, I cried for the people in that bathroom with him, and I cried because it was unfair that hate that powerful could ruin so many lives. I didn't care what someone had poetically said at the Tony awards, I didn't care about the national conversation regarding moments of silence versus action, or radical extremism versus homophobia, I only cared about him, this young man who knew he was going to die and had to tell his mother that.

Our reaction as a society is to jump into cause and effect mode. We are all shocked, we are all angry, and saddened, and heartbroken and I wonder why that cannot be enough. Why can't we all just allow ourselves to feel those things without creating more things to be upset and divided over? Why are we pouring salt in our wounds and calling it antiseptic? Why can't we just mourn the death of 50 people and the rising reality that there are too many people and things in this world willing to die because they believe that their beliefs are the right ones. Isn't there space to just reflect on how every step towards justice brings about moments where injustice happens more and more frequently. We have to live with ourselves, we have to explain this to our children, we have to call our parents and tell them we love them because that could have been any of us gunned down and we should allow at least 24 hours to do that.

… It could have been any of us, that's what stuck for me. I had joked on date a few nights before about how much more I enjoyed Gay clubs to straight ones because I got to "dance, feel fabulous, and feel safe. That morning on my way to brunch I was mentally reminding myself to text my girlfriends about going out to San Francisco in 2 weeks for Pride weekend. There would be dancing, there would be fabulousness, there would be the amazing feeling of having a whole city moving to the "Pulse" of living life as whoever you wanted and loving whomever you wanted. Now, after this, each Pride and every LGBT nightclub will be a little less bright, a little less happy, a little more defensive in how they chose to live their lives. If that's not the sad moral to this story, I don't know what is.

11

Stop Telling LGBTQ People How We Should Be Responding To The Orlando Attack

Mitch King

In the wake of the tragedy in Orlando, an interesting conversation has emerged. There's a dialogue between the idea that all Americans should be affronted by the attack and the idea that this was an attack intended to terrorize and silence LGBTQ voices during a celebration month specifically for them.

"So what?! I'm just as scared of that possibility as anybody else! Stop trying to take ownership of the tragedy. 'You people' politicize everything."

"We" only politicize things that matter in a political context. Unfortunately, the world has made the person I choose to love a political issue. So yes, I suppose "us people" – that is, your brothers, sisters, cousins, parents, children, neighbors, coworkers, and peers – do indeed politicize everything.

Sorry.

I will, however, continue to politicize it.

Until I don't have to answer questions from prying strangers about my sexuality.

Until I can walk down the street in Anytown, USA holding my boyfriend's hand without you taking a second glance.

Until I can adopt one of the many children without parents without jumping through acrobatic hoops and fielding lawsuits from insert-organization-here.

Until I can use the same bathroom as others without you caring what my down-there looked like when I was born.

Until I can claim the will of my husband without his family claiming that my marriage wasn't real since we weren't a "normal" couple.

Until I can pick my child up from school without having to justify why she has two dads.

Until I can go to dinner with my husband and child without you stopping at our table and asking "who does she call 'daddy' then?"

Until I can ride the train home after a date and share a kiss with my boyfriend without you saying "I don't want my kid seeing that."

Until I can walk down the street without you calling out slurs and your friend apologizing: "Sorry, he's just drunk." As if that is any justification.

Until I can rent an apartment with my boyfriend without you insisting that we're just roommates.

Until I can have straight friends without you insisting I must have a crush on them, "because, you know."

Until I can speak about my boyfriend without you insisting I tell you "wears the pants" or which one of us is the "pitcher."

Until I can donate blood to help in a tragedy that directly affected my friends and neighbors without you dictating my celibacy.

Yes. I will politicize it. Because we can't afford not to politicize it. You have made sure of that. So yes, I will take ownership in the attack. It should be an affront to all Americans, but next week you'll have forgotten that this was a deliberate hate crime, and the status quo will continue. For me, however, my reality will remain rooted in fear of going to a club because "what if somebody comes in and tries to do a copycat attack?"

I'm scared. And that's a shame.

12

Here Is What The Manager Of Pulse Nightclub Had To Say About The Attack

Jacob Geers

Sunday morning, the nation was rocked as news arose that Pulse Nightclub — a gay bar in Orlando — was attacked by a terrorist with multiple firearms. At the end of the day, over 50 people are dead and many more were injured.

Brian Reagan is a manager at Pulse Nightclub. Starting as just a patron, he eventually became an employee, and later still, he became the manager. In a heartfelt Facebook post, Brian talks about his experience at Pulse and his feelings about the horrendous terrorist attack:

Brian Reagan 🌀 feeling heartbroken.
7 hrs · 🌐

To all my friends, family, and loved ones. People I've known for years or just met. I moved to Orlando in 2004 Pulse nightclub was the first Gay Club I ever went to. I instantly fell in love with it. The atmosphere, the expectance by everyone. The first time I could be myself as an open gay man of 18 years old. Over the years my love never faded. I have had the amazing opportunity to become the Manager of the building for the last 2 years and help create and continue the amazing legacy that Pulse was based on. I am forever and will always be forever grateful for the Orlando Gay community both inside the Pulse Orlando building and elsewhere. We may be a "Big City" however our community is a family. We all treat and take care of each other, we all know each other(this is largely why I've stayed in Orlando for the past 12 years) The events that took place on Saturday evening into Sunday morning I will never forget. I was fortunate to make it out of the building with a few scrapes and bruises. Many of my Orlando based Family, Friends, and Loved ones were not as fortunate. I am absolutely sick, sad and at a loss of words for what is still transpiring. We are a family, we are all friends, and we do all share One Pulse. I love you all so very much. It seems as if a horrible nightmare as the names on the list are released. The one comfort is I can recall an amazing story of love ,fun, and smiling nights together, laughing and dancing the night away. Please my Orlando friends and Family stay strong with me for yourself and for the world. Our friends, our family will never be forgotten.

-Brian Reagan
Pulse Orlando Manager

Facebook

Brian reminds us, that despite the evil in the world, the forces of good always find a way to love and take care of each other. Peace to those we've lost, and strength to those who endure.

This horrendous attack will not soon be forgotten.

13

Why Gay Nightclubs Are Such Necessary Places Of Survival To The LGBTQ Community

Madison Moore

Every gay person I've talked to about the massacre in Orlando has expressed feeling numb, cold inside. Shocked. There's an element of randomness in terror attacks, the overall marketing strategy being that relentless killings can happen to anyone, anywhere, at any time. No place is safe. This is, anyway, what vigilantes want us to think, and the uncertainty of when and where is partly what causes the feelings of numbness in the aftermath of an attack. It forces you to think about your daily rhythms and the small, last-second decisions you make to be or not be somewhere. A change in route, a change in plans. You "could have been there."

This time, with an attack on a gay club, a place that is supposed to be a safe haven, a place to go when there's no place left, the feelings of numbness have to do with the fact that many gay folks look forward hitting the club on the weekend.

"I was at a gay club when I got the news," one friend told me. At the gay club we're pouring the drinks at the bar and we're turning on the fog machine and we're spinning music in the DJ booth and we're working in the coat check and we're lip synching in full regalia to eternity. We go to gay clubs to dance, drink, meet new people, let our hair loose and ultimately to find our queerness, to find ourselves.

Orland could have been any one of us.

I love nightlife and I always look forward to going to the club. I'm never sure what's going to happen, and that's sort of the point. We shave, we get dressed up, we put on cologne and perfume and we become our best selves. We flirt and we kiss and we love.

Clubbing is resistance.

I've spent thousands of hours in nightclubs over the course of my lifetime, and I can say that some of my most memorable experiences have happened while I was shouting to someone over loud music in a nightclub. Gay clubs were the first spaces I learned it was OK to be gay in, a place I could sneak to in college without my folks or even my roommates knowing. When I came out to my cousin Katrena as a late teen I made her go with me to a gay club in East Saint Louis — *made* her in the sense that I didn't have a license so I couldn't get there by myself. I had to bribe her with White Castle. We had a blast and I bought her one of those huge, oversized dildos at the club's giftshop as a joke. She loved it.

With gay pride celebrations popping off in cities around the world, and as we think about those we lost in Orlando and process our numbness and exhaustion at the reality and frequency of gun violence in the United States, to say nothing of hate crimes and the fight for equality, we must remember that gay people and spaces, including nightclubs, have always been under attack. Sometimes the attacks are legal, like laws that ban gay people from even congregating openly in social spaces in the first place. Other times the attacks have much more force, like when a bomb exploded in a lesbian bar in Atlanta in 1997 and when another went off at the Admiral Duncan in London's Soho in 1999. Not to mention Stonewall in 1969.

As ever, clubbing is resistance.

Queer nightlife is always about survival, community and resistance, not booze and boys in boxers dancing on light boxes (though it's about that, too). A place of refuge. Queer nightlife is a safe haven when no other place seems safe enough, when walking down the street holding your girlfriend's hand could get you killed. Queer nightlife matters because it creates a space, perhaps the only space, where it's possible to be yourself, to realize you're not alone.

We have to keep loving. We have to keep dancing. We have to keep being fucking fabulous.

14

I'm Tired Of Watching Humans Die Just Because Some People Really, Really Like Their Guns

Jacob Geers

I try to avoid editorializing whenever I can. I prefer to give a platform to other people's ideas and thoughts, allowing competing ideas to bounce off each other and form a larger conversation that I can curate and watch from the sidelines.

But, I've 100% had it with watching my fellow humans die because the United States lacks proper gun control.

Last night there was a shooting at a gay club in Orlando. When all is said and done, there will probably be roughly 20 people dead. As of right now, we don't know who is responsible and what their motive was (though we can probably guess). But here's the thing: it doesn't matter.

Because we will forget. We have a week of grieving, we will promise each other in Tweets and hushed conversation that something will change — but it won't. We'll all go back to work Monday, talk to our colleagues about how tragic the shooting was (as well as the shooting of vocal talent Christina Grimmie) and then pour ourselves another water at the water cooler and send Karen the memo she asked for. Then we'll forget, and it will just blur into the other 172 shootings we've had in the United States this year. It's all so much. It's all too much.

The National Rifle Association (and friends) have more power than our tears, than our tweets, and our prayers. Despite almost 90% of Americans being in favor of universal background checks, the NRA only has to move the marionette strings attached to the hip of ~~our~~ their politicians, and nothing gets done.

And why? Why, why, why?

Because their right to own a M134 Minigun, or flamethrower, is more important than your life, than my life, than our children's lives.

HUFFPOST POLITICS

It's not a matter of national security, or civil rights, or anything else. It's just some people really, really like guns.

It's not a national security issue. *Not* having gun control is the national security issue! If anything else in America — say birth control or condoms — caused even one death in America, we would rally to fix the problem in a hot second. Just think about the Ebola "crisis" when two people in the United States were diagnosed. We could barely talk about anything else, because it was a clear and present danger to our safety. Guns are somehow immune from scrutiny — because, ya know, "freedom"!

Allow me to be perfectly clear: If you have to fear for your life every time you walk outside the door, because an unknown gunman may shoot you down — I don't care how many guns you own inside — you are not free.

It's not a civil rights issue. On every single other right in our Bill of Rights, we have accepted reasonable limitations and regulations. You cannot run into a crowded theatre and yell "FIRE!" You have the right to own a car, but you must prove you can drive it. You have the right to be a salesman, but you cannot lie to your customers. You have the right to protest, but you cannot be violent. The NRA and gun lovers, however, tell you that "what we have now is working" (at the price of 228 dead this year alone) and that ANY further action is Obama trying to steal your guns!!!!!!!!

Which, by the by, under President Obama, more guns have been sold than any time in our nation's history. The President himself, perhaps because of this, has consistently gotten "F" ratings from key gun control organizations — like the Brady Group.

Gun rights activists aren't here because of national security or civil rights, they are here because they really, really like their guns. And like many other trending issues of today — such as LGBTQ+ equality — they are reluctant to change and are clinging to what they know. Their attitude is strengthened by the NRA, which has a financial incentive to stir up paranoia about guns to energize their base. This has the added benefit of jacking up gun sales, which gives healthy profits to their friends in the gun industry.

See how messed up this is?

Throughout the history of our country, a lot of Americans have died. They have died during various civil rights and labor movements. They have died while protecting our country in wars. Today, victims of gun violence are dying because some people really, really like their guns.

Yes, there have been instances where gun control has failed, and the bad guys have gotten the guns anyway. Nobody is claiming that there is a foolproof solution that will serve as a silver bullet. It may come to light that the attack on Pulse nightclub would have happened regardless, or some other excuse for why guns aren't relevant in this event. But we have to stop relying on anecdotal evidence. We have to start fighting the trends. We have to try something. We have to do something.

Inaction is only rarely an American response to a serious problem, and we don't wear it well. When explaining his plan to help in World War 2, President Franklin Roosevelt said, "If you're neighbors' house is on fire, you don't haggle over the price of the garden hose." You put out the damn fire, and figure everything else out later.

Our country is on fire. And, and as imperfect as it may be, we need a garden hose. We can't forget. We need to do something. And as voters, we need to make our ballots weigh heavier than the NRA's coffers. And we need to do it today.

15

Those Who Are Missed. Those Who Are Remembered.

Jacob Geers

These are the names of the innocent human beings who died in the June 12th terrorist attack on Pulse Nightclub in Orlando, Florida. The victims ranged from 18 to 50. They all had so much ahead of them, needlessly cut down by hate and homophobia. To the families and loved ones, all we can offer is our love, condolences, and the hope that something, soon, will change.

Stanley Almodovar III, 23 years old

Amanda Alvear, 25 years old

Oscar A Aracena-Montero, 26 years old

Rodolfo Ayala-Ayala, 33 years old

Antonio Davon Brown, 29 years old

Darryl Roman Burt II, 29 years old

Angel L. Candelario-Padro, 28 years old

Juan Chevez-Martinez, 25 years old

Luis Daniel Conde, 39 years old

Cory James Connell, 21 years old

Tevin Eugene Crosby, 25 years old

Deonka Deidra Drayton, 32 years old

Simon Adrian Carrillo Fernandez, 31 years old

Leroy Valentin Fernandez, 25 years old

Mercedez Marisol Flores, 26 years old

Peter O. Gonzalez-Cruz, 22 years old

Juan Ramon Guerrero, 22 years old

Paul Terrell Henry, 41 years old

Frank Hernandez, 27 years old

Miguel Angel Honorato, 30 years old

Javier Jorge-Reyes, 40 years old

Jason Benjamin Josaphat, 19 years old

Eddie Jamoldroy Justice, 30 years old

Anthony Luis Laureanodisla, 25 years old

Christopher Andrew Leinonen, 32 years old

Alejandro Barrios Martinez, 21 years old

Brenda Lee Marquez McCool, 49 years old

Gilberto Ramon Silva Menendez, 25 years old

Kimberly Morris, 37 years old

Akyra Monet Murray, 18 years old

Luis Omar Ocasio-Capo, 20 years old

Geraldo A. Ortiz-Jimenez, 25 years old

Eric Ivan Ortiz-Rivera, 36 years old

Joel Rayon Paniagua, 32 years old

Jean Carlos Mendez Perez, 35 years old

Enrique L. Rios, Jr., 25 years old

Jean C. Nives Rodriguez, 27 years old

Xavier Emmanuel Serrano Rosado, 35 years old

Christopher Joseph Sanfeliz, 24 years old

Yilmary Rodriguez Solivan, 24 years old

Edward Sotomayor Jr., 34 years old

Shane Evan Tomlinson, 33 years old

Martin Benitez Torres, 33 years old

Jonathan Antonio Camuy Vega, 24 years old

Juan P. Rivera Velazquez, 37 years old

Luis S. Vielma, 22 years old

Franky Jimmy Dejesus Velazquez, 50 years old

Luis Daniel Wilson-Leon, 37 years old

Jerald Arthur Wright, 31 years old

www.ingramcontent.com/pod-product-compliance
Lightning Source LLC
Chambersburg PA
CBHW050511290526
45786CB00007B/2520